Card is in back of book.

MOVIEMAKING

MICHAEL L. LEVINE

MOVIEMAKING

A GUIDE FOR BEGINNERS

CHARLES SCRIBNER'S SONS
NEW YORK

Acknowledgment is gratefully made to Linda New Levine, my wife; to Iris Brand; Robert Chesler; Arnold Greene; Barry Levine; Ana Rosa Ojeda and other students at The Pablo Casals Intermediate School in The Bronx, NY; and to Joseph Petrella, principal, who created the atmosphere for educational innovation that inspired this project.

Library of Congress Cataloging in Publication Data

Levine, Michael L
    Moviemaking.
    SUMMARY: Outlines the steps involved in making a movie using Super 8 film from the initial planning session to the premiere.
    1.   Cinematography—Juvenile literature.
[1.   Cinematography]   I.   Title.
TR851.L48   778.5'3   80-19314
ISBN 0-684-16707-7

CONTENTS

Part One
GETTING STARTED

Moviemaking can be fun.

But what must be done before you can use a camera? The first thing you can do is read this guide. Then you can begin to *plan* your movie.

Start with a planning session. Write all of your ideas on a planning sheet.
Try to put them in the correct order:

What comes first?
What happens next?
Where does it take place?
Who are the stars?
How does the story end?

Get to know your camera. Read the instruction booklet that came with it.

The salesperson who sells you film probably will be able to answer
any questions you have about the camera.

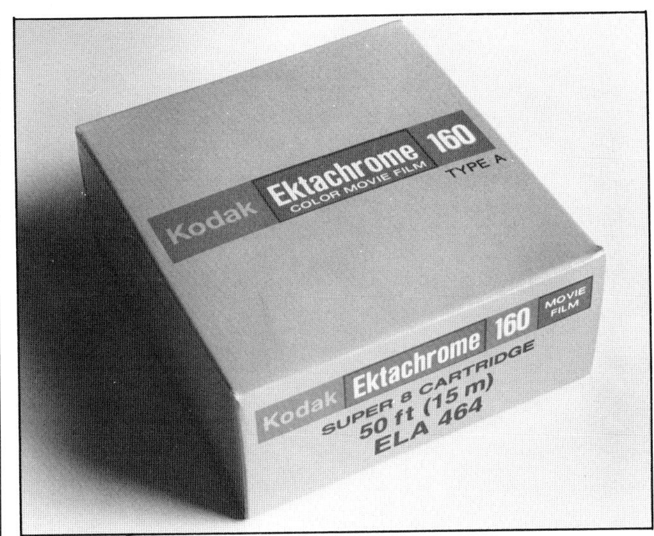

Decide what type of color film will be best for your movie, indoor or outdoor. If your movie will be shot outdoors, any Super 8 film will do. If your film will be made indoors, use Kodak High Speed Ektachrome 160 Super 8 Movie Film. With this film, special lights are not needed; just turn on all the lights in the room.

If your camera is equipped with an electric eye, it will automatically adjust for each lighting situation. If it is not so equipped, read the instructions that came with the film and set your camera accordingly.

Attach your camera to a tripod to avoid "camera shake." Tighten the tripod so that the camera is rock-steady.

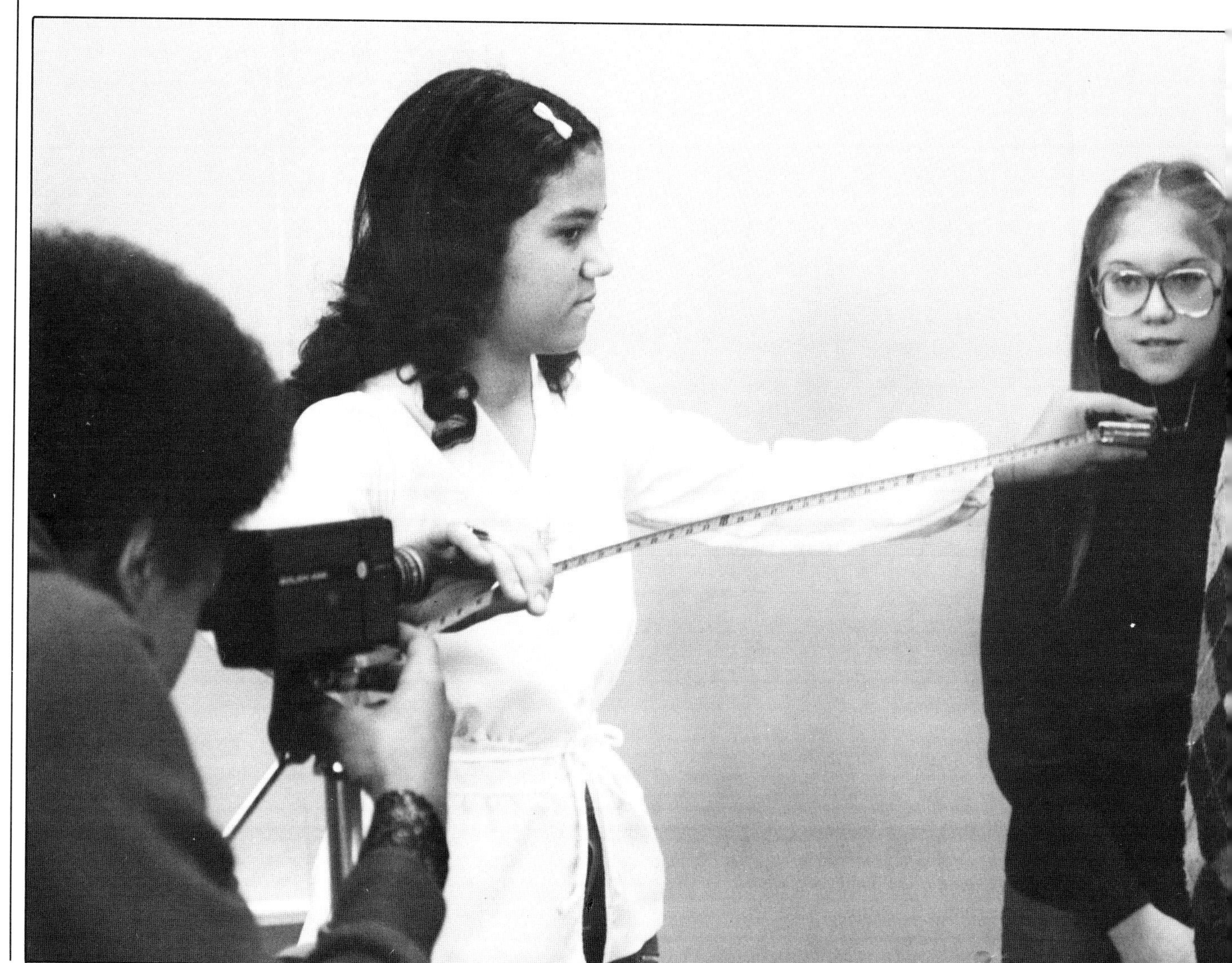

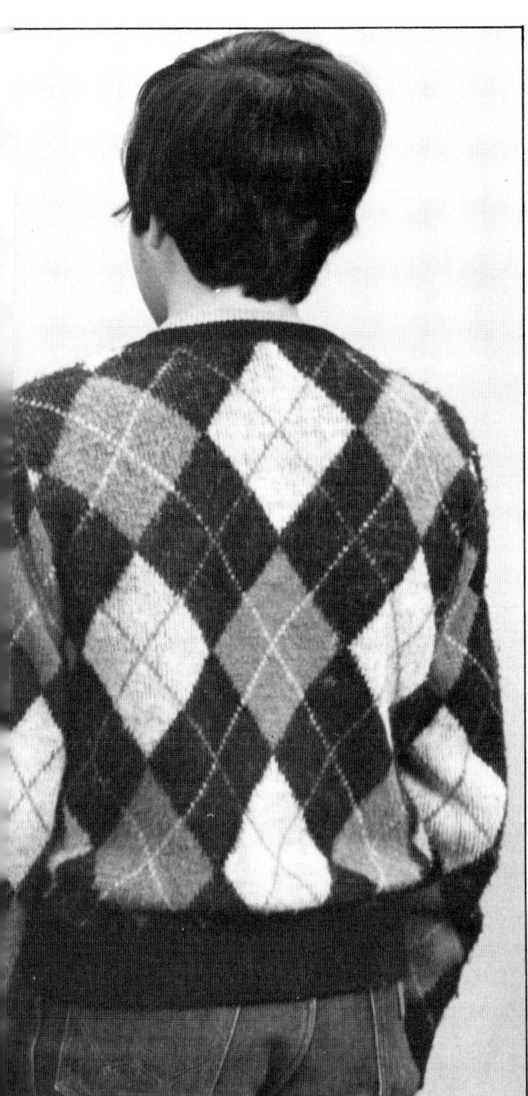

Measure the distance to the subject and set this distance on the focusing ring of the camera lens. Otherwise, your subject will be out-of-focus.

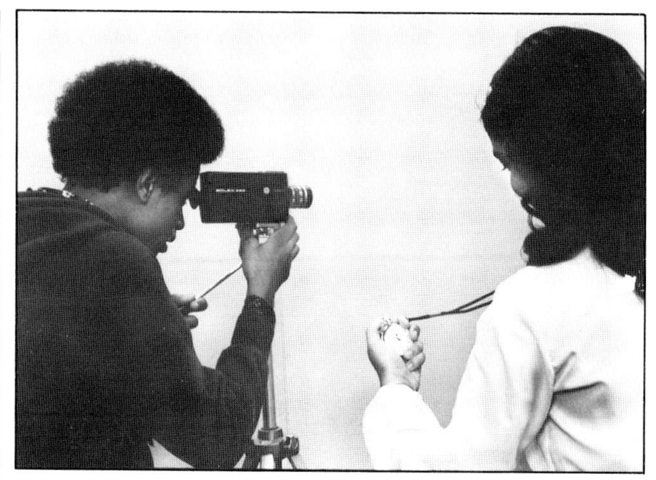

Rehearse each scene before filming. Keep the scenes short. Use a watch to time each one. A roll of film lasts only 3 minutes and 20 seconds (200 seconds). Time your rehearsal so as to be sure that you have enough film for your ending.

You are almost ready to begin filming your masterpiece. Remember, the more time you spend in precise planning, down to the last detail, the better your film will be. In your planning, be sure to include details of camera position and camera movement, as well as techniques to change location and show the passage of time. These techniques are covered in Part Two.

Part Two
CAMERA! ACTION!

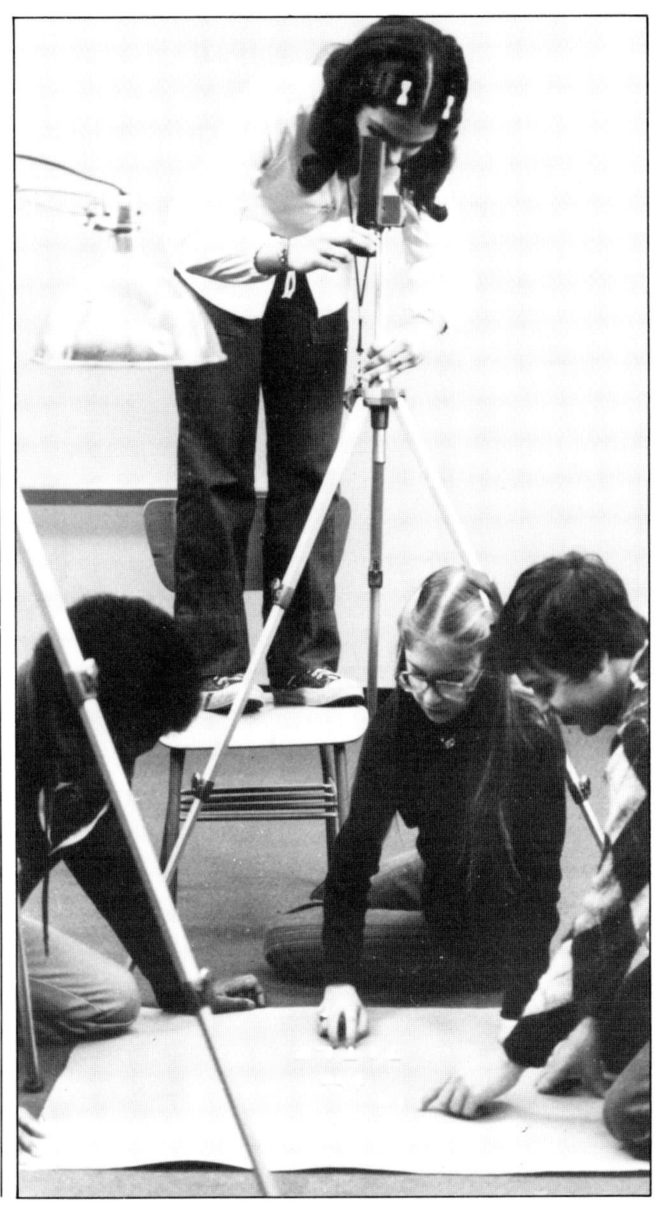

With film in the camera and lights pointed at the subject, carefully film your title. Pull the camera's trigger for twice as long as it takes to read the title. Don't forget to include names of the writers and producers of your film. List the actors and the parts they will play. Remember, use both first and last names. Think of all the titles and credits you've seen in the movies and on TV. Use your imagination to create something special.

There are several ways to present words; handwriting on paper or chalkboard is not easily read by your audience. Try plastic letters, or wooden blocks, or letters sold in photography stores. In art supply stores you can buy rub-on or transfer letters to make a more individualized title. Since you are using color film, try using color in the title.

Before you begin to film, practice different types of shots.
Learn to use the camera in various ways to achieve specific effects.

Where will the camera be? Must it be so far from the action?
Move it closer. Move it very close.

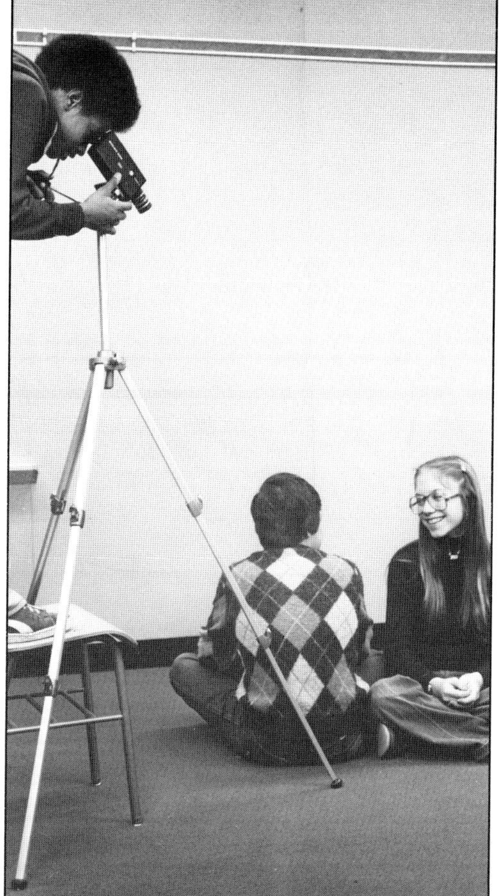

...or high near the ceiling. Does it make a difference in the picture?

Try placing the camera low to the ground...

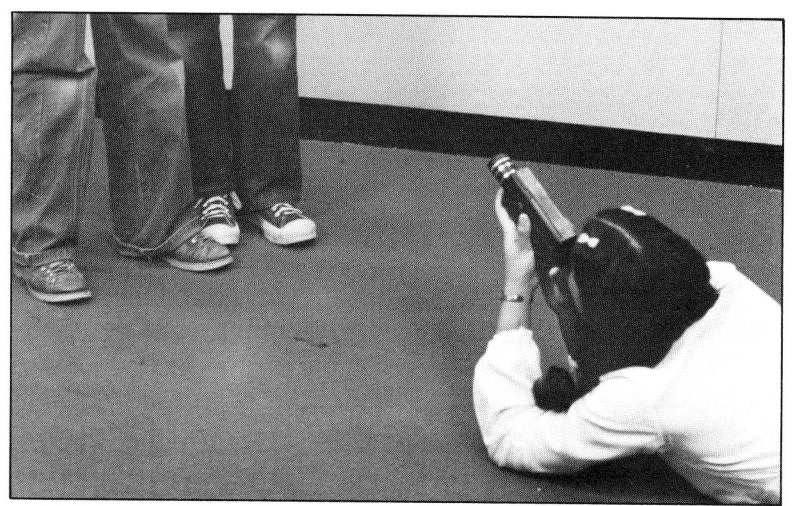

Move the tripod and camera to vary the camera's position. Don't always take a "normal" shot.

Try something new!
Change
the distance.

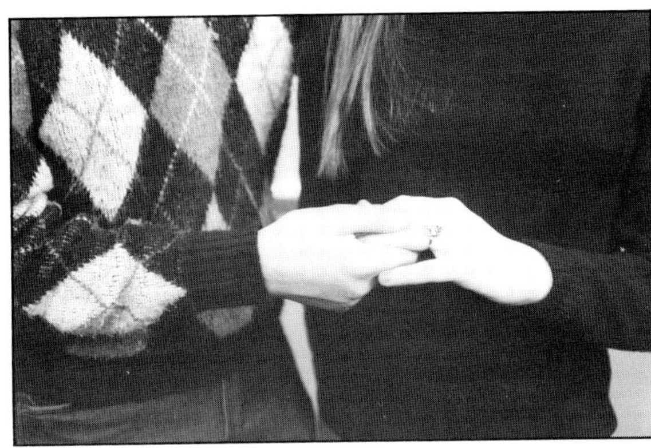

Don't stay in one place.
Occasionally get close—
or even very close.

A good rule-of-thumb might be to change the camera's position for each scene—and a scene should usually be not more than 15 seconds.

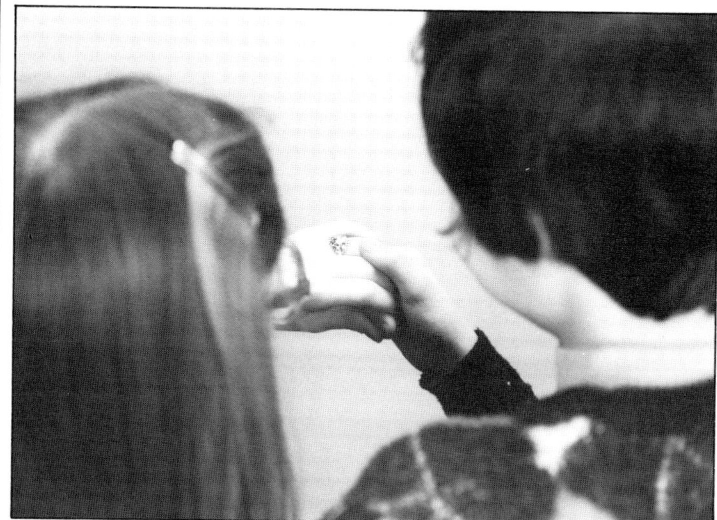

There are different ways to shoot the same scene. Select the best ones for your movie.

You can move the camera while you are filming a scene. Caution: too much movement will make your audience dizzy! Move slowly! Move rarely!

Try the camera's zoom lens, or slide the tripod closer to the subject while you film.

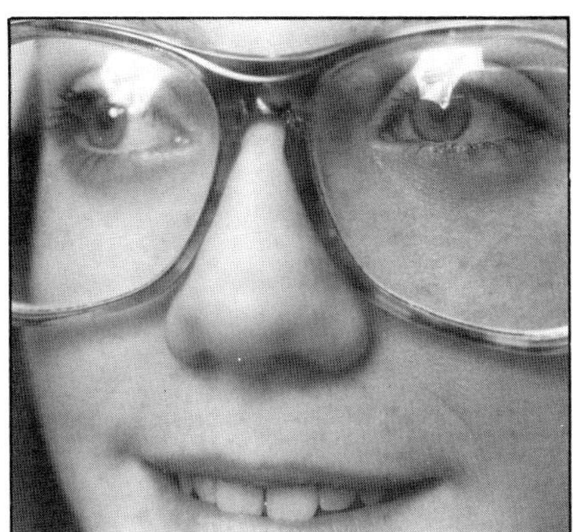

Using the tripod's pan head, swing the
camera to the right or left to follow the action.

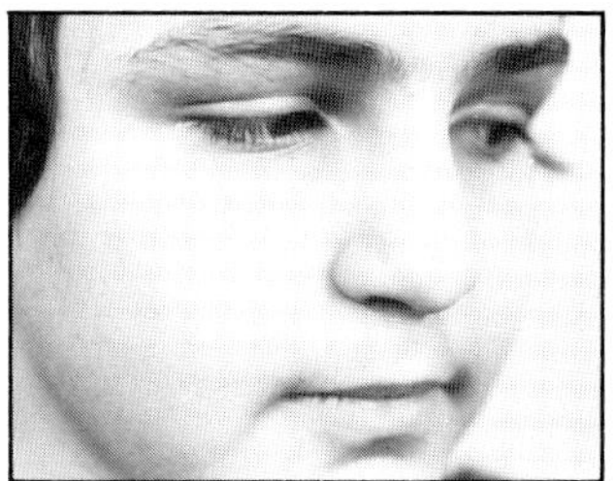   

Tilting the camera up or down while
filming could add interest to a scene—
but use this technique sparingly.

You are almost ready to begin your movie. But how can you show the passage of time, or a change in location, or even that two events are occurring simultaneously? There are several techniques that you can use just like a curtain at a stage play. Practice all of them and incorporate your favorites.

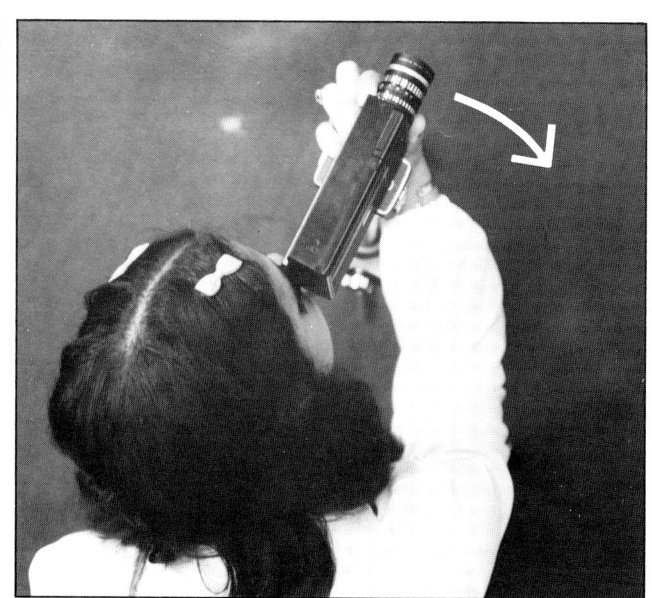

One technique—the quick pan—can be used several ways. With the camera on its tripod, swing (pan) the camera quickly to the right at the end of the first scene and then stop filming. To begin the second scene, start off swinging the camera to the right and finally land on your subject. Use this technique to show simultaneous action or a change in location or a change in time.

Another technique—the vertical wipe—lowers a card (curtain) in front of the camera lens to end scene one; the second scene begins with the card slowly being raised to expose the lens.

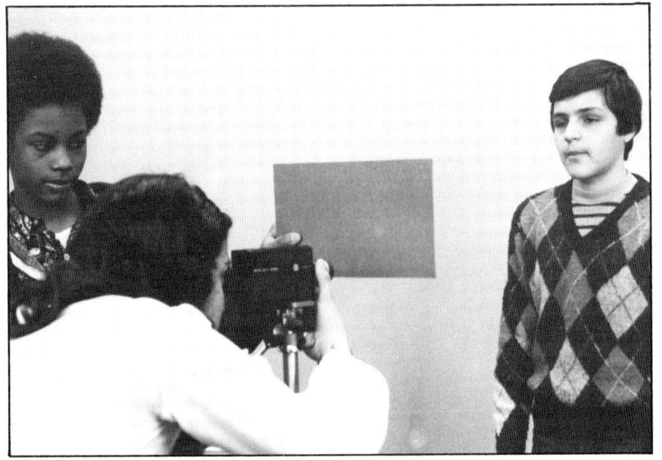

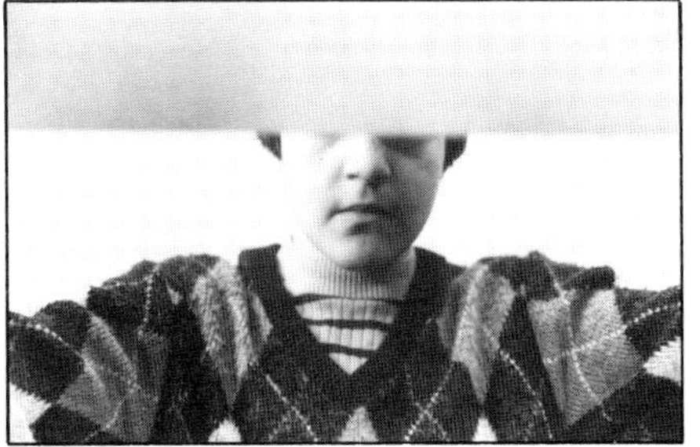

A similar technique—the horizontal wipe—covers the lens from the left to end scene one and uncovers the lens to the right to begin scene two.

Of course, when the lens is covered completely, the camera is turned off.

Fancy combinations of the vertical wipe and the horizontal wipe can add interest to a movie with many scene changes.

Still another technique—the blur-out—
may be used with cameras that must
be focused. End scene one by completely blurring out the subject. (If the
subject is close to the camera, focus on
something far away; if the subject is far
away, turn the focusing ring to the clos-
est setting.)

Scene two will begin with the subject
completely out-of-focus and then slowly
coming into focus.

The close-up change is used when one actor changes location between scenes. At the end of scene one, move in very close to show the actor's face.

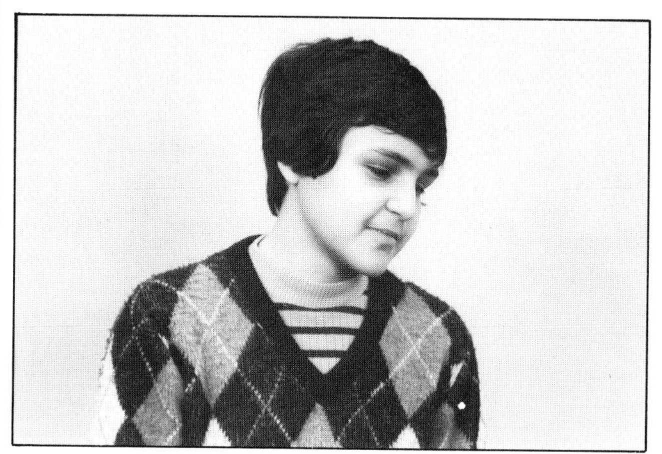 

Begin scene two in exactly the same way you ended the first scene.
The change in location becomes apparent when you back away from your subject during the beginning of scene two.

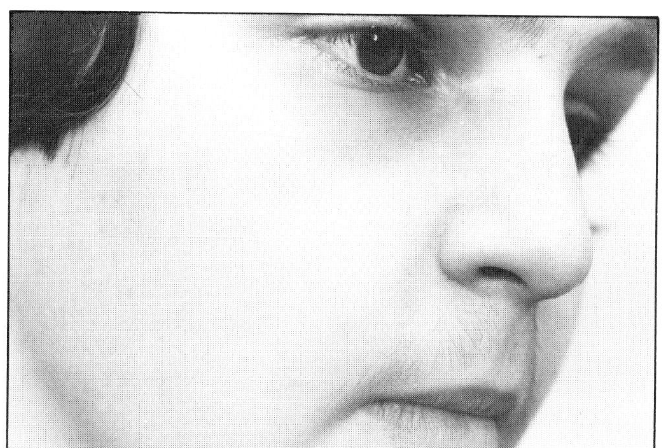 

The most often used scene change—the cut—is also the least interesting and could confuse your audience. At the end of scene one, stop filming.

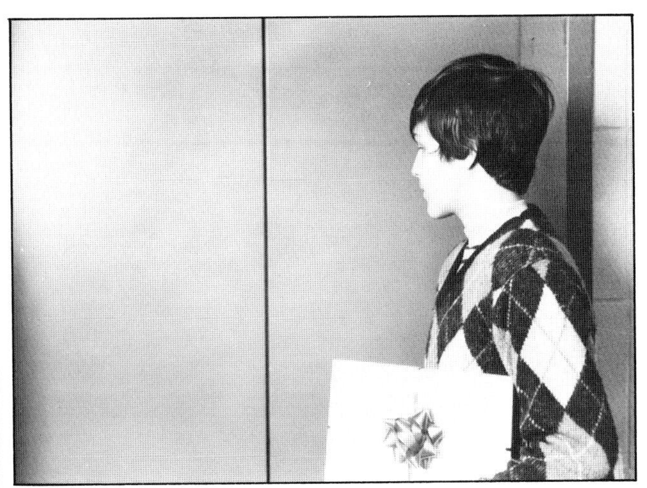

Then change location and begin scene two.

Now, make your movie! Follow your plan and include all of the filmmaking techniques you have learned. Take it slow, and enjoy yourself!

When your film is returned from the photo processor, there will be many things to do before your audience can see it. The techniques of editing, splicing, and adding a sound track will be covered in Part Three.

Part Three

FINISHING TOUCHES

Welcome back. By now you've completed the first parts
of moviemaking—planning, rehearsal, timing, and, finally, the actual use
of the camera to shoot your roll of film. The film has been returned from
the photo processor and you're eager to see it. So gather together
all of those involved and set up your projector.

The first showing is for enjoyment. The actors will be looking for themselves, and there probably will be much nervous laughter. Now show the film a second time. Watch it with the following aim: *What can we do to make it better?* Which parts could be cut out? Would it be better to switch the sequence—scene one, scene two, scene four, scene three, etc.? Where would narration help? What about background music?

Editing changes and improves your film. It's almost like getting a second chance to plan. During editing, scenes that are repetitious can be cut out, scenes that are too long can be shortened, scenes that are too short can be combined with other scenes, and scenes can be arranged in a new order. Once you've made a detailed plan (in your editing planning session), you simply cut the film into parts, rearrange the parts, throw out the parts you don't need, and put the whole thing back together again. (The last part is called splicing—and it's quite simple. If you can tape things together, you can splice.)

An editor-viewer (a hand-cranked projector with a built-in screen)
makes the job simpler, but editing can be done on a projector. First, write
down a description of scene one, scene two, scene three, etc. Using a
grease pencil, place a mark on the film where each scene starts.
(The grease mark wipes off easily when you're finished.)

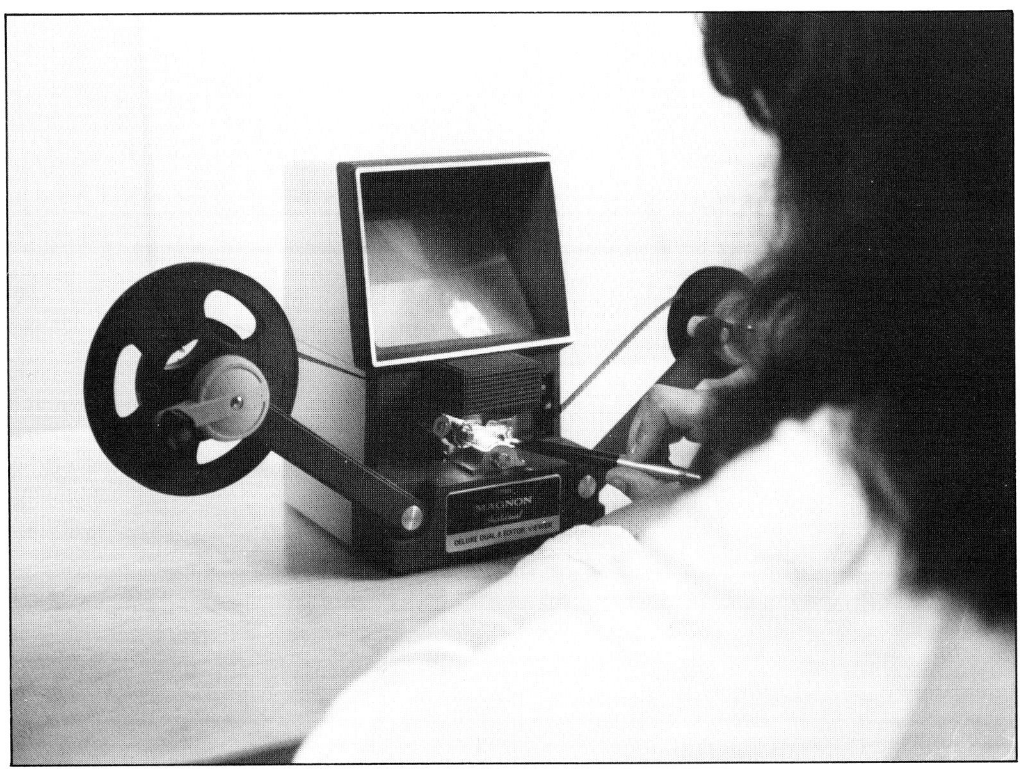

Decide on your "editing script" what should be cut, switched, or shortened. Rearrange the film parts in the correct order. Using spring-type wooden clothespins as clips, hang the new scene one on clip #1, the new scene two on clip #2, and so on for the entire movie. Fill your wastebasket with "out-takes." Be ruthless. The shorter you make your film now, the better it will probably be.

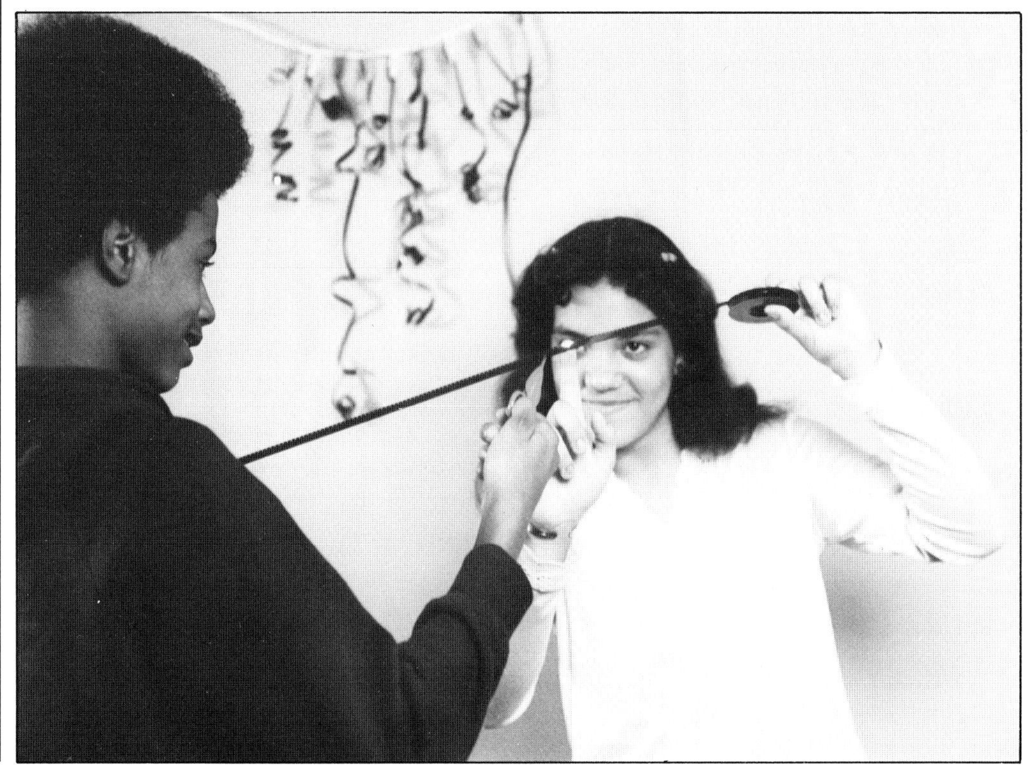

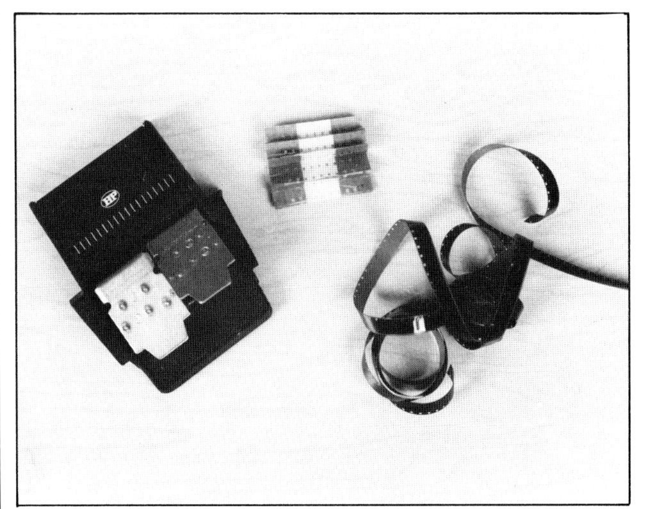

Now you will need a splicer—perhaps you can borrow one from the school AV department or camera club—splicing tape, and some "out-takes" for practice. The important thing to remember, in splicing, is that the tail of each piece of film must be cut exactly to fit the head of the next piece. Then simply apply the splicing tape and rub it down.

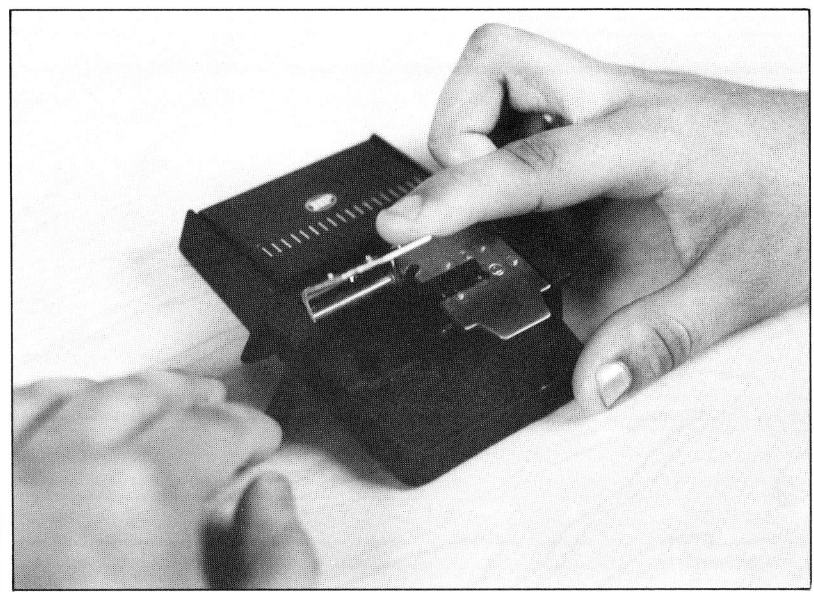

Avoid handling the film too much; wear splicing gloves if you can get them. Fingerprints are very difficult to remove from film.

Cut the film and splice it back together again.

When the film has been completely edited and spliced, project it again to check for mistakes.

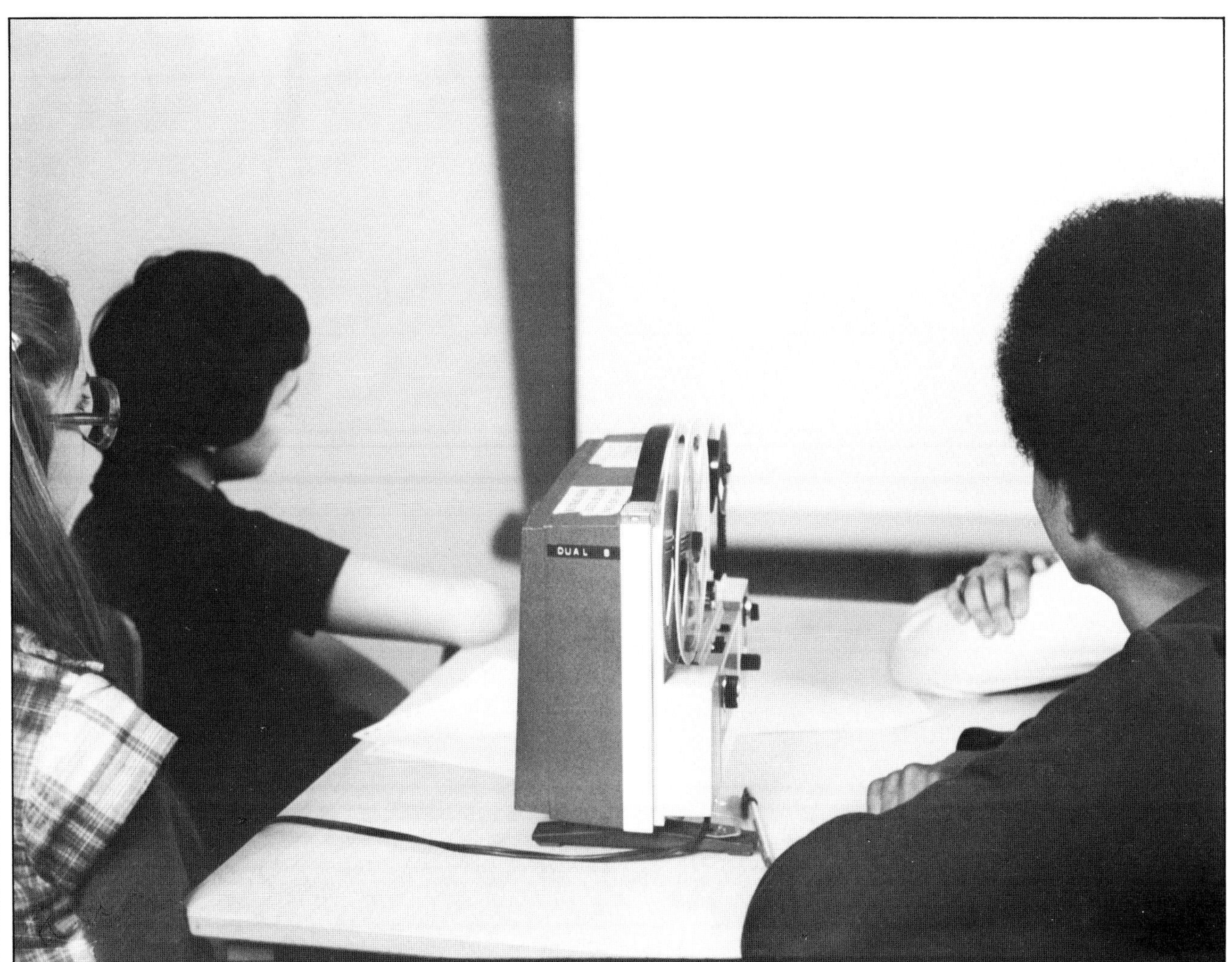

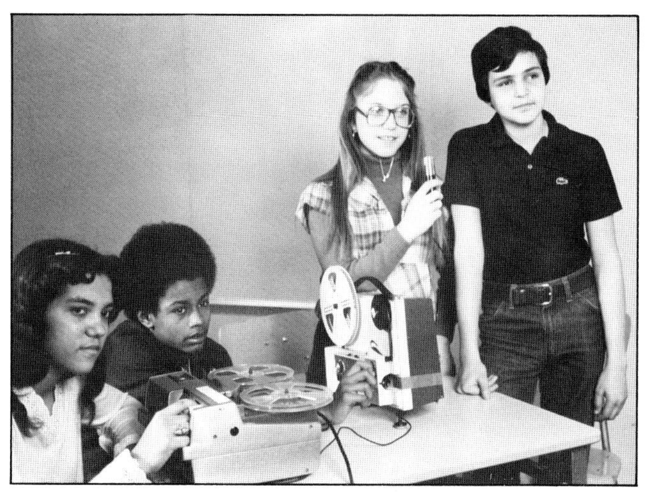

Now, while viewing your film, decide what narration is necessary for audience understanding. You do not have to tell the viewer what he is seeing; give only information that expands the viewer's comprehension. Ask yourselves what background music will add to the viewer's enjoyment of your film.

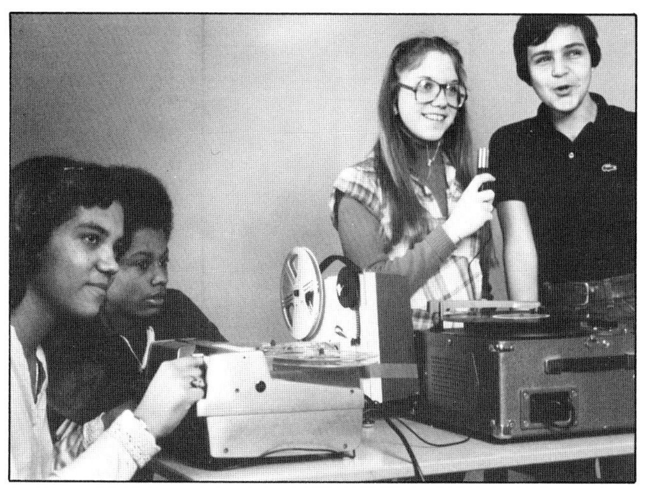

Using a tape recorder, and a phonograph or tape recorder for the background music, record the soundtrack while watching your film. Try to keep the microphone as far away from the projector as possible. Begin your tape with a hand clap when the picture starts, so that you'll always be able to match up the picture and sound.

Now view the film while listening to the sound track. Satisfied?
How can you improve it? Could you cut more from your film? How can
you improve the sound track? Are you sure that this is the
best you can do? Yes? Then your film is complete and you're ready
to announce the first public showing.